Racism Without Racists

The Truth About Immigration
True Stories of Discrimination, Abuse, and Exploitation

Cristina G.

Copyright © 2017 Cristina G.
All rights reserved.
ISBN: 9781973213000

To Gene, whom I owe my life and the fulfilment of my dream
&
To Martine, my dearest friend, who believes and supports me every day

***

To those who cry in silence,
I understand your pain,
I wish you to find peace,
And people with a soul.

Breathe, Read and Love.
Visit authorcristinag.blosgpost.com and join the writer who cares.

Contents

Prologue 1

Fifty shades of nude 2

A village girl in a big world 20

Slave at the end of the 20th century......................... 39

From the frying pan into the fire............................. 55

Great Expectations, Charity & Condescension 78

Please, don't cry papa 96

Also by Cristina G. 103

About the Author 104

Connect with the Author.. 105

Prologue

This short book was written with the genuine intention to donate all the earnings to a worthy organisation at the services of victims of any sort of discrimination.

As I didn't have a specific charity in mind, a month ago, I spent days looking for the right one. There are so many!

I took a few names down and wrote some emails explaining my selfless intention.

None dignified me with a response.

I am not sure what to make of this. I cannot say that I am disappointed or upset. After everything I've been through, this only proves what I refused to believe for so many years: my nationality defines me.

I won't mention names or point fingers. But it's hard to accept that any associations that challenge discriminations by default could do exactly what they should fight against.

The following is my true story. A story of many... too many. Is it yours too?

Fifty shades of nude

I was twenty-four when I left my homeland for the first time.

Where too?

Italy, one of the most beautiful countries on earth.

Everything I knew about Galileo's nation was learnt from a couple of TV series: *La Piovra – Octopus* and *Edera – Ivy*. I fall in love with the language which I thought (still think) is the most melodic of them all.

From these popular serials what I gathered most was that people get shot in the daylight by the mafia.

I left convinced I wasn't going to come back alive or that I'll see any of my family members ever again. It was like going on my last path. I took the risk anyway.

Why?

Because I had no other choice. I needed to look for opportunities. And if that meant that I was going to be killed by a random mobster, 'then be it.' I thought in my head and put my mind at peace. 'I would rather die in the pursuit of a better life, then drown in hopelessness.'

I remember my parents' expression of utter despair. The countless tears and the out-loud prayers. I wasn't the first to abandon them, half of their children – five out of ten – were very, very far away.

Romania is the country I was born during one of the most oppressive communist regimes ever existed.

When the communism fell, in December of 1989, we all gained freedom. The worst part is that we didn't even know we were caged for all those years.

But freedom was not as we pictured it. If before, the TV programs were sparse and the movies were censored, suddenly, we were watching naked people having rough sex in front of others. The shock of my parents was planetary.

We were catapulted in Sodom and Gomorrah – the famous two cities mentioned in the Book of Genesis. The divine punishment was upon us. We were going to burn on earth before burning in hell for eternity.

I... couldn't even look. My father never watched TV since then. With the passing of years, my mother got used to it. She doesn't even blink when she watches countless scenes of unrealistic nude in her favourite telenovelas.

I was 13 at the time, and I had no idea of what was going on. I never left my village before. Nobody ever told me anything about sex. I've never seen a couple kissing, not in real life and not on TV. I couldn't ask anyone because you see, I was raised a Catholic. We went to church every day, sometimes even twice a day.

We didn't even dream asking questions like that.

We didn't use to treat reprehensible acts like that.

We didn't have sexuality lessons in school.

There were no magazines or tabloids.

The internet… was not yet invented for us. I couldn't even imagine how PCs looked like.

My parents never kissed or hugged, at least I never saw them doing it. They didn't even sleep in the same bed. To the day I wonder where, when and how they managed to conceive twelve children on these terms.

I was addicted to reading. It was my favourite pastime. I would have read ad infinitum if I could. Except that I needed to help my family with the land and the animals. I only had the nights at my disposal. I read books, thousands – at the light of a candle – but they didn't treat sexuality. They were probably censored too.

Never in my life, I witnessed anything so morally questionable broadcasted on TV at any hour of the day and night. I was a farmer's daughter, all church, work and studies, those scenes confused and disgusted me, to be honest. My naivety was limitless.

The first video music we saw was Lambada. Do you remember the colourful outfit of people – especially women – the short skirts and the exposed thongs every time they spin, the explicit looks, and the happy and movement dance?

Don't you still blush and perhaps feel aroused watching it now, after all these years?

Well, the people we used to see on TV were Nicolae and Elena Ceausescu mostly. Daily. If the transmission lasted for three hours, one and a half was with and about them. Sometimes, even more than that. They were fully dressed in elegant attire, smiling, but highly formal. They didn't hold hands, hugged, or kissed. And they didn't go to church. But I will write about this later.

With the black and white era, everything was in fifty shades of grey. So I don't remember the colourful outfits, and I thank God for that because I watched it now and it's even more explicit than I remembered. To tell you the truth, I had no idea they wore those bright garments until at the time of this writing.

So you see, nothing that resembled turpitude was shown on TV before the December of 1989. No horror movies and no soap operas either. No games, no competitions, no songs with double or triple entendre messages. Everything revolved around the two leaders of the country. They were shown happy, motivated, and on the side of people. Except they weren't.

Ceausescu had big dreams for its small country. I am sure he didn't mean to bring it to its knees. I am sure his intents were good and honest. And I am sure he had no idea how bad we were living. He was probably unaware of the fact that we didn't have heat or hot water in our homes. Or that we spent nights in the rain waiting for the shops to open so we can buy a litre of milk or a piece of bread. I refuse to believe that a human can sleep well knowing that children work the land to pay the debts of the country he made so irrationally.

He looked like a good guy, and I listened to him when he used to stress so much on education. "Study and Study and Study Again to become great humans," he used to shout with vigour while raising his right punch up in the air.

How could a man say that he loves his nation and ignore the despair in our eyes? He probably didn't know because he had a purpose: to put Romania on the world's map. He dreamed of his nation being recognised and appreciated because he knew how strong and capable his people are. Romania's history is great. Inventors, composers, poets, writers, and many artists died and remained unknown to the world just because we are people of inferior birth.

But you don't think that about us – immigrants I mean. Do you? I know. We live on a racist planet without racists. Isn't it?

On the 25th of December 1989, Ceausescu and his wife – Elena – paid with their lives for all these major oversights.

Four days before – on the 21st – Ceausescu gave his last speech in the Revolution Square. During this oration, he belittled the revolts in Timisoara, the people and the reasons behind them. Utterly unaware of the state of mind of his nation, he sounded calm and candid. That was when people reacted. They had enough. The limit of acceptance was crossed. Romanians knew they were risking their lives, but there was no present, and most definitely there was no going back.

In total disbelief, the dictators ran and hide. Still, he had the time to give the order to shoot to kill. But the soldiers refused to obey.

"It could be my father or my brother in there," they said while the one in command put a bullet in their body.

The next day, the tyrants were hunted and captured like animals. It was truly humiliating, and if you saw the look in their eyes, you would have burst into tears. They were terrified. But we were on our knees. We were cold and hungry. And we didn't think straight. We wanted them to pay for all those years of utter indigence, censors, and exploitation. We wanted them out. We craved for freedom, oil without the ration book and… oranges.

Nicolae and Elena Ceausescu were not religious people. They didn't like competition. They were the only Gods on earth. For them, Christmas didn't exist.

But for most of us, 1989 is the year in which Christmas was covered in blood and sunk in bereavement.

On the 25th of December 1989, in a small room in front of a kangaroo court, they were judged and sentenced to death. Ceausescu refused to accept the officiality of the court. He answered no question and demanded to be judged by people – by *his* people – convinced that they loved him.

But the kangaroo court judges were deaf and intransigent. Shooting was the chosen method. It wasn't difficult to find shooters. Hundred volunteered. At that time, every single person in Romania – from children to elderly – would have pushed the trigger in a heartbeat.

The entire process was broadcasted in the world. If your read *Oranges at Christmas in a Communist Country*, you know that my family and I shed countless tears. We were heartbroken. We just couldn't accept the fact that humans can kill other humans with such an unthinkable cruelty.

A conspiration theory

Forgive me if nowadays I double with the horrible thought that this process was a huge mascaraed. A coup d'état architected in detail by some mighty people in the world.

Nicolae Ceausescu was the ruler of a state that paid all its financial debts on time. His country owed nothing to anyone at that time. Probably an unprecedented situation and the magnates of the world couldn't allow that.

Romania had countless hectares of forests — uncontaminated fauna and flora, fertile lands and well-established agriculture, colossal industry system, waters with healing properties, strategic location on the map. The president refused to be too friendly with other communist sharks or conservative presidents. He didn't bow his head, and he didn't sell his country short. He wanted to be the absolute and supreme leader of his country alone in the world. He tried to make Romania great. Some couldn't stand that. The supremacy is not a given right for someone so ambitious and… unworthy.

Ceausescu was almost illiterate. One of the nine children of an extremely religious farmer, at the age of eleven, he ran away from home and got into shoemaking. His boss was an activist of the Communist Party – illegal back then. It was just a matter of time until Nicolae joined him. Because his background was gloomy, Nicolae – still a kid – did everything in his power to distance himself from it. Allegations were made, there is the suspect that his father was an alcoholic and abused him, his siblings, and his mother in many ways.

With outstanding determination and grit, Nicolae made a huge name for himself. From shoemaker to president. If this is not an extraordinary, tell me what is then?

We didn't know his true story at that time. We had no internet and no freedom of speech. Ceausescu wasn't proud of his past and family. He didn't want anyone to know he was born a peasant and abused by a religious extremist.

Despite his lack of education, he was not dull-witted. On the contrary. Now that I know this, I admire and respect his genius.

But that doesn't take the fact that somewhere along the line, his humanity vanished. I don't know if it was the love of power, the sufferance, the anger that blindfolded him. He lost or choose to bury his sight and empathy.

Deliberately or not, he imprisoned his people and watch it burn without blinking. He gave orders to kill anyone who refused to obey and respected his commandments. He took lives based on rumours and allegations. He suffocated the spirit of the nation he wanted so badly to make great. He kept his people in utter deprivation and ignorance and demanded ovations and gratitude in exchange.

He thought he was a God, *he made* himself a God. He took churches down and abolished faith. He chased priests, peasants, writers, inventors, and random geniuses and threw them in real prisons. He gave the order to torture and let them die on the freezing-cold cement floors.

Christmas was erased from the calendar. We were not allowed to use the name *Christmas* in public: schools, workplaces, meetings, parties. The most precious celebration of the year was referred to as "Winter Festivity." Santa Claus was Father Frost.

There was no Halloween or Easter, of course. No bunny, no chocolate eggs, no treasure hunt.

Is his religious father the one to blame for Ceausescu's aversion towards religion? I don't believe that one can be held accountable for the abominable acts of others. His father might have been a despicable person, but he didn't put a gun to his son's head and said: "Be a God, hold them in your power. Keep them in the dark. Make them starve and crawl. You are their righteous owner."

Ceausescu took all these appalling decisions by himself.

As farmers, we were slaves on the land that belonged to us. I witnessed how my mother in her knees cried and begged to be allowed to keep a piece of land her mother gave her. That happened every year around March. It was excruciating. To the day I still see her tears rolling down her beautiful face, and her calloused trembling hands reaching out like she was a beggar.

My parents had ten children, and we needed more food than most families. We worked from dawn to sunrise to make an honest living, but we lacked all essential amenities.

Hot water, electricity, central heating were timetabled.

The food was rationed like during a war.

Children had no toys, no chocolate, chips, or chewing gum.

Women knew nothing about makeup, high heels, and branded clothing.

Men couldn't even imagine how many car models were out there; how many types of cigarettes, cologne, and jeans existed.

We were prohibited to go to church and pray to an invisible God.

Travelling outside the country was inconceivable.

We had no cartoons, telenovelas, reality shows or Hollywood movies to entertain us.

No games to play. No social networks to mingle.

But mostly, we had no exotic fruits. No oranges, no bananas, and no kiwi.

We partnered with the oppressors I believe. Because we suffered very much when they were assassinated. My octogenarian parents lived the

World War II. They saw many dead people. Still it hurt so badly when the shooters pushed the trigger. All of us cried inconsolably for hours. Christmas was covered in blood and horror. Baby Jesus was not born that night. Instead, two people were shot dead without a fair trial. There was no Christmas tree, no songs of happiness and triumph. Only pain and tears. We went to bed with a hefty burden on our shoulders. A burden that many of us are still carrying after more than twenty-eight years.

We had no idea we were finally free because we didn't know we were prisoners. We thought that was normal life everywhere around the globe. They kept us in absolute dark and ignorance. Nevertheless, we suffered for them. Because they were like us. Humans. Except they lost their humanity many years before and they didn't even know they did. They were monsters of egoism. Everything revolved around them. They had the monopoly on absolutely everything.

We were like marionettes: clapping, cheering, jumping and speaking on command.

We ate what they gave us.

We watched and read what they decided.

We wear the clothes they thought were appropriate.

We washed when they gave us permission.

We had no plans and no future. We were dead people walking by inertia.

In the communists' eyes, we were all equals. Except we were not.

There is no such a thing as equality when some pay a higher price than others. When a few have less than most although they work longer hours and harder.

Communism is a utopia. An outstanding concept in theory, but in practice is pure and utter exploitation of the masses for the success of one single man, woman, or party.

Communism is a prison. The minds of people are on a leash. The intellect is kept low on purpose — "The more you know, the more you want. You need to succumb and be happy with little."

The soul is caged — "There is no other God than me. I am the only one that can help you. The power is in my hands. I have the right to kill as I ponder. You are at my command."

The eyes are blindfolded – "You live in the most beautiful country in the world. The richest and the biggest. You don't need to go anywhere else. This is heaven."

The desire is a sin – "The clothes you wear are modern. The movies you watch are the best. The music you listen is the top. The food you eat is tastier than in any other part of the world."

Work ennobles man – "Slog for the country, for the greater good, not for you and your family. You already have everything you need. I provide for you "

My first memoir entitled *Oranges at Christmas in a Communist Country* narrates about this period. Read it.

Nowadays we want Ceausescu back because freedom is not at all as we thought was going to be. We crave for the good old fifty shades of grey.

Actually, we don't really. We just want opportunities, jobs, high education, politicians who work for us, not who steal everything they put their eyes on. We want a future for our children and grandchildren, basic amenities for our parents, and a roof over our heads.

But mostly, we want to... stay home.

A village girl in a big world

As I mentioned at the beginning of the first chapter, I left my country seventeen years ago.

It was August of 2000 when I packed a few things and abandoned the only reality I knew. For two years I have tried to get a Visa. I was denied twice, but I couldn't give up. There was nothing for me in my country.

After the communism, Romania went into total chaos.

The forests got denuded almost instantly like people were waiting at the frontiers for Ceausescu to be taken down.

How much time before the killings the rest of the world knew that Ceausescu had the days counted? We had no idea.

The entire industry system collapsed at once like it was built on sand. If during the communism almost all Romanians had a job, suddenly most became unemployed.

Many high schools were closed like someone out there wanted us not to have a proper education.

We had no idea where to go, and what to do. But we were used to studying that we loved very much, and we thought we had the right to higher education. I had to go to a college and follow courses I didn't like because I had no other choice. My dreams of going to the university vanished.

All brands of alcohol, cigarettes, clothes, cars invaded at once and conquered the hearts of Romanians kept in indigence for so many years. But we had no money as we had no jobs anymore.

Hundreds of TV stations were created almost overnight. They broadcasted everything under the sun. We were bombarded with soap operas, reality shows, pornography, songs with angry messages that instigated to violence, rebellion, and decadence.

The freedom of speech was misinterpreted, and everybody fought and verbally abused everyone.

Countless political parties popped out like mushrooms. But at the power was Ceausescu's ex-right hand. Surrounded, of course, by many – if not all – of his former staff.

> "Days go past, and days come still,
> All is old and all is new,
> What is well and what is ill,
> You imagine and construe...
>
> ......
>
> With the selfsame scales and gauges
> This great universe to weigh,
> Man has been for thousand ages
> Sometimes sad and sometimes gay;
> Other masks, the same old story,
> Players pass and reappear,
> Broken promises of glory;
> Do not hope and do not fear..."

These are verses from *Gloss* (1883) by Mihai Eminescu – the greatest Romanian poet the world ever heard of.

If you remember, I was born a farmer in a village. Besides the four years of college in a city situated 60 km away from the place of my place of birth, I never travelled. I knew nothing about the world or my country for that matter. The communists taught us a fabricated history. I doubted of everything. Except for mathematics, chemistry and physics, potentially everything else was fiction. Even geography, anatomy, and biology. Probably not the last two, but I couldn't be sure, so I did my best to erase or write the latest information on top of the old ones.

Today I dare to think with distress that maybe even the books I read were censored or incomplete stories. It doesn't really matter because I read others.

Romania is a Christian state with 18 religions and denominations. 81% of Romanians are born and raised Orthodox. But my family belongs to a Catholic community from Moldova, a region situated in the North-East of Romania.

At this point, you might be wondering how can I affirm that I used to go to church even twice a day when Ceausescu prohibited and persecuted religions. All of them with no discrimination.

It's a fair query.

Ceausescu was born an Orthodox. I had reservations that he persecuted religions because his father was a bad person as many had claimed. To support my theory, there is the fact that after his parents passed away, he ordered to build a church in their honour. I incline to believe he was an atheist by choice and persecuted every person or thing that undermined his absolute authority. The fact he demolished churches is a causality. He just wanted to build something else in their places. Bad luck.

Nobody ever forbade my family and me to go to church. We didn't bring up religion or nominated God in public, but we were not harassed for our faith.

I was a true believer and practised religion by choice. God was the one I used to turn to when my mother was humiliated and exploited. I often woke up at 4am to participate to the first service of the day. Not because my parents forced me, but because I wanted to. I prayed with fervour and felt elevated by the songs of hope and happiness. I followed and respected the rules even if often I questioned many.

What I never questioned was why Ceausescu didn't celebrate Christmas. Things were like that when I was born, so it wasn't my business. I thought it was normal. I didn't know better.

I never used or heard foul language during the communism period. My parents were very strict about it.

One day I came home from school – I must have been seven – and bluntly asked my mother what a word I never heard before meant. My mother was working at the weaver. She blushed and made me promise to never pronounce that *bad* word again. And I didn't.

To the day I am unable to use foul language in my mother tongue. I have no problem cursing in Italian, French, Spanish, English, and other random languages.

Do you know why?

Because they don't sound dirty to me. My mother doesn't blush when I say them out loud because she doesn't understand them.

As far as I am concerned my existence in Romania before the age of twenty-four, was more and less like in an Amish community. Simply life, plain closing, no technology, and church.

As I mentioned, it was August of 2000 when I abandoned the only reality I was familiar with. That day was one of the saddest of my life, after the Christmas day in 1989.

My parents cried in despair. I was convinced I will never see them again, so were they.

I was shy, with little self-esteem – none really – uncertain of everything. The world was huge and I wasn't interested in visiting it. I just needed to find a purpose.

A priest and nun helped me. They found me a sponsor in Italy who vouched for me so I could get a visa. They arranged a trip to Michelangelo's country and took me with them. When they came to get me, it felt like going to die. I wasn't curious, I wasn't happy, I wasn't even able to cry. My senses were petrified.

The religious people were used with travelling. They spoke a perfect Italian, and they knew the road. I tried to look and sound excited. I pushed myself to cheer and exult every time something unusual appeared on the horizon. Half a day later, I was exhausted. But the worst was yet to come.

I knew I was blessed and I felt guilty. After the communism, I watched documentaries that narrated about people who traversed the oceans in old boats – wrecks – in the pursuit of a future only to starve death. Or drown before the final destination, maybe robbed and killed by unscrupulous creatures. They paid heavy money for the trip made in inhuman conditions. They slept one on top of another on a wet pavement alongside fish, garbage, and perhaps dead bodies.

A nephew of mine crossed the Alps at night and walked for thousands of kilometres to reach Prosecco's land only to be caught and get an interdiction on his passport. He lost thousands of euros. Money he didn't have.

After a thorough interrogation on a very personal note, the priest decided to give me Italian lessons. I should have been grateful, except I wasn't. I just wanted to be left alone with my reflexions like an animal wounded to death. Then we prayed and recited the rosary over and over and over again.

The level of exhaustion rose to the sky. Previously to the trip, I couldn't sleep well for months. They thought I couldn't wait to see the world. I... thought I was going to die.

I have no recollection of how long it took us to get to the Italian frontiers, probably 24 hours. My senses were still in lethargy, but I was tired, and all I wanted was to sleep.

1 km before the border, the priest – who was also the driver – stopped the engine. I didn't question why. I was a passenger. He turned to the nun and had a brief discussion. They both got off, went to the back of the car and opened the trunk to look for

something. Then I was invited to step out of the car too.

The nun had a long look at me and put a veil – like the one she was wearing – on my head. I thought it was a joke and started laughing even if I didn't feel like it.

They joined me but said it was no joke.

"We thought it would be safer if you wore this veil. Italians are very respectful of men of God. They will allow us to pass faster and without any issues if this car was filled with nuns and priests."

"But I don't have a tunic. I am wearing trousers. What if they ask me to step out of the car? Can I have a tunic too, just in case?"

"We didn't bring one. Only the veil."

"I look ridiculous," I said in apprehension.

"No, you don't! You have an angelic face. Don't worry. They won't ask you to step out of the vehicle. It's disrespectful."

"I have a visa. Why do I need to pretend I am someone else? It's a sin and illegal. I could get arrested. We could all get into trouble."

"You watched too many movies, girl," said the priest amused. "We will not get into trouble, and you are not going to hell for this. You're a good Christian. Relax."

But I couldn't relax. Many things happened in my life that lead me to believe I was a very unlucky person. That visa was the only good thing that happened to me until then. I feared the worst and I prayed with desperation.

From my father, I unconsciously acquired to worry about everything. I was terrified of breaking the law. My heart was racing, and my eyes were blurred with tears. There was a storm inside my mind. With inhuman efforts, I appeared calm and serene. I even smiled when the custom-house officers looked at me. They smiled back and waved at us to move along.

It turned out that the clerics were 100% right. I wanted to cry so badly to release the devastating tension, but the men of God laughed and mocked on my desperate expression.

I found it cruel, but I knew they were not able to understand my state of mind. I never left my village for more than a few days. I never spoke with a policeman or crossed a border before. For them, it was fun, for me was torture.

Everything was scary. The oxygen I breathed was pure fire. It burnt my throat and my lungs. I wanted to go back. I wanted to work the land and help my parents. I wasn't ready to affront the world. I was twenty-four, but I was just a child. An innocent and naïve child.

However, the reason I embarked on that terrifying experience in the first place was to help my parents. To offer them basic amenities and to repay them for so many sacrifices they made for all their children. I needed to stay strong and pretend to be happy. No, not happy, ecstatic.

Our first stop in Italy was in a motorway café – autogrill. I have never seen one before. It was huge. The sun was bright, and I peered inside from the windows.

The ecclesiastics observed my odd reactions with amusement. I stared at doors, there was no handle. I had no idea how to open them. They burst into laughter. Then the doors magically opened like someone's said: *open sesame*. I felt stupid as I still had no idea how that mechanism worked.

They thought I was amazed, but I was just… frightened. And I felt so guilty for not feeling what they were expecting from me.

A temperamental restroom

I asked the nun if she knew where the toilets were. She told me to follow the crowd. A group of women got in, and I gathered they were looking for the same ladies' room, so I followed them. They spoke a different European language, probably Bulgarian. Some of them were young, some not so much, but all seemed equally excited.

The toilets looked like cubicles. Of course, I saw them in my country too, but there were so many in the same room. I waited patiently in line listening to the sound of flushes and words I couldn't understand. When my turn came, I felt like going into a confessional box. I closed the door wondering if I was going to be able to open it again as the mechanism looked quite complex.

I relieved myself paying a lot of attention not to touch anything that didn't belong to me. I was afraid of getting diseases. My sister is a nurse, and she instructed me since I was little to be very careful when I go to public restrooms. I cleaned myself as well as I could with baby tissues I bought from Romania.

Then I looked for the button that activated the flush. It wasn't where I expected it to be. I looked everywhere for it or a handle, a chain, or anything else that had that purpose. There were none of these things. There was only the toilet. I looked under, I stepped on the pavement thinking it had a sensitive spot somewhere. Nothing. I heard laughter and animated discussions every time somebody got out of the cubicles, but I couldn't understand a word. I was sure that they had the same weird problem I was facing.

Five minutes later, I was sweating cold because I didn't figure it out and I couldn't leave without cleaning the toilet. I waited until everybody left and I got out in tears thinking that I am the stupidest person in the entire world. When I opened the door, the flush activated itself. I felt the urge to scream and kick, but I abstained myself. The mechanism was connected to the door and that I've never seen before.

I went to wash my hands. I found the soap, but there was no water coming out from the taps. But I knew there was water because I saw the other women washing their hands. Once again, there were no buttons, handles, sensors. I touched and moved the pipe a few times. Nothing. I sighed and took the bottle of water I had in my bag and rinsed my hands. Then I stepped on something, and the water came out.

At the time of this writing I find it hilarious, but at that moment I all I could feel was concern.

'How am I going to get all these things? What if everything has a different method of doing? What if every mechanism is unique and complicated? It seems like a mouse trap. I am a village girl, I will never survive in this big and complicated world.'

My eyes were stingy. I looked in the mirror and blinked a few times to send away the tears. Then I washed my face with cold water. I left without drying my hands. I was suffocating, I needed some fresh air.

The nun was waiting for me impatiently. "What took you so long?" she asked.

"I couldn't find the flush and... Never mind. It's all good now. I learnt something new."

She laughed, I smiled... grimaced more likely.

"I faced the same issues the first time. You'll get used to it in no time," she confessed.

"Why haven't you told me? I never left my village before. I don't know anything about the world," I said upset.

"Come on now! It's fun, isn't it?"

'Only for you,' I replied in my head.

I sighed. I knew she couldn't understand. It wasn't her fault that I felt so inadequate, so scared and alone in the universe. I didn't want to be there. I wanted to be home, in my village with my parents, and sleep in my bed.

The nun suggested looking around while the priest was ordering some pizza. I wasn't interested at all, but she was observing my every reaction. I had to put on a mask of exhilaration. I felt like I owed her.

She expected me to behave like a child in front of blue ice cream, but I never liked ice cream.

I had no money so I couldn't buy anything. I looked without seeing, pretending I was amazed when all I wanted was to cry and sleep.

Then the priest called on her mobile. We joined him at a table near the window. A few seconds later, our orders arrived.

Now, I have seen pizza before. I went with my mother and my siblings to eat quite a few times in the city near my village. But this was different. First, it was huge and very thin. Then it was... empty. There was little cheese and some tomato puree. In Romania pizzas used to be half in size, thick and extremely rich: salami, a lot of cheese, olives, peppers, etc. The exact opposite of the one in front of me.

Although I wasn't hungry, or excited, I pretended I was. I clapped my hands while my eyes got bigger. My reaction pleased them. I felt like Pinocchio, and I touched my nose to see if it grew longer. Luckily, it remained the same. Big.

I pushed myself and prayed to God to help me deliver what they were hoping for, but I couldn't eat more than one slice. I was happy it had none of the ingredients I mentioned earlier. I couldn't have eaten more than one bite in that case.

"Oh. That's disappointing. We were convinced that you were going to devour it all," said the priest. "We ordered the pizza just for you."

I feared that they were going to say that. I swallowed air while I was sweating cold, trying to find a good excuse besides the real ones: I wasn't hungry. I didn't want to be there. I wasn't fond of pizza.

"I am so sorry, but I have nausea. Maybe it's from the trip. I never travelled for this long. I am very grateful though. Thank you. God bless."

They glanced at each other and smiled at me. I smiled back thinking that I was the biggest liar in the entire universe and God will punish me severely for that.

When they finished eating, we gathered our things ready to leave. Suddenly, a loud beeping resounded in the autogrill. A shopkeeper – or whatever they are called – asked a person to step back from the door. He demanded her to go with him showing her the way.

I heard that noise many times in Romania's new western shops. Sometimes those devices beeped with no reason. I have been in that situation a couple of times, and it wasn't nice. I got scared and started to tremble. I didn't want to be searched in my bag. I have changed my underpants while in the restroom. Plus I had pads and... other stuff I didn't want others to see.

The priest looked at me and almost rolled on the floor laughing his socks off. For both was very comical, for me was terrifying.

He pushed me towards the door chortling. I walked praying harder than Papa. 'It's going to beep. I know it. I am so unlucky. Help me, God.'

It didn't though. The tension was so high that I thought I was going to crash on the pavement.

They found that utterly exhilarating. I think it was, but not for me.

We got inside the car, and for another three hours, we prayed at unison. Then we've reached our first destination: the house of my guarantor.

Slave at the end of the 20th century

I didn't know he was my sponsor when I've met him for the first time. I thought the priest, and he were friends. And they were, still are. His elderly mother was so nice and so happy to see both the nun and the priest. She hugged me too, and I felt grateful. She seemed such a nice person.

It was love at first sight between my sponsor and I. Ironically, I've never believed in such a thing until then.

We ignored the mutual feeling – not that I was 100% convinced he felt the same that moment. Only later he confessed. In a couple of days, I was destined to go and work as a babysitter. Besides, I didn't even know if he was married or gay. Or a psychopath.

The priest and the guarantor acted together to find me that job, and it only came up a few days prior to my arrival. Nobody asked me if I wanted to be a babysitter, but I needed a job.

The family *I was delivered to* was a wealthy one – quite famous in the area. The woman was an authentic blue blood descendent – a countess or something. I really don't know what, nor that I cared. For me, she was a human just like me. For her, I was a starving animal.

When I got there a girl from my country who used to work for the countess, was waiting for me. She resigned from the job but was instructed to prepare me for the role of babysitter. I asked her why she was leaving.

"I found another job," she said.

"For how long have you been living in Italy?"

"Three months."

"Oh. And you are already leaving the job. May I ask why?"

She laughed and said, "You'll see."

The girl remained for another two days I think. She showed me where the things were, taught me how to use the washing machine, dishwasher, and other devices. We didn't speak much because there was no time and because the patron didn't like hearing us talking.

The room I was given was in the basement. The walls were covered in mould, and it smelled like damp. It was terribly humid. I could barely breathe. I asked the girl how she managed to sleep in there.

"I didn't. My boyfriend came every evening to take me to his place."

"I don't think is healthy. My father used to say that one could die because of the mould."

"Only if you are allergic to it. Are you?"

"I don't know. I've never slept in a room like this."

"I guess we'll find out soon then."

I didn't like the sound and the prospect of that statement. I was okay with the probability of ending up shot in the head by a mobster, but not with suffocating in a cavern.

I had no other choice though. I wasn't going to complain. Besides, complaining to whom?

The aristocrat lady couldn't stand the sight of me. Every time I was near her, she yelled to keep the distance. She called me names: illiterate, peasant, primitive. I really didn't know what she was blathering about. I was neither of those things. I went to college, I read a lot, I was an educated and respectful person. I wasn't sure she saw me as a human. I believe she imagined I was a sort of a monkey.

I was trying to learn Italian. One day, while cleaning – the two little children were asleep – I was writing a word on my hand because I couldn't remember it. The lady boss caught me, pulled the pen out of my hand with incredible rage and ordered me to go to the bathroom to erase the blue ink from my skin.

"You didn't come here to learn Italian, you philistine! The only reason you're here is to work because you were starving in your petty country! Don't ever dare to do this again!"

She seemed possessed. Her reaction scared me to death. I understood then why the previous babysitter left after only three months.

I went to bed crying and praying. I doubted that I was going to last that long. In eight days I couldn't eat anything. Anything at all. I was too stressed. I didn't have time to adjust to the new country's canons. Things happened too suddenly. I abandoned hope and opportunities, I just wanted peace.

When the lady informed me that we were going to fly to Rome from Venice, I saw my chance of escaping the nightmare.

I've never put my foot in an aeroplane before. But I often heard that they go down, and many people die at once. I used to be terrified of the thought. Not that day though. A plane crash was my only salvation.

A friend of the noble drove us to the airport. When we got there, the lady put the youngest – a girl – in my arms and gave me one of the suitcases to carry. I've seen that happening in movies. I was a maid. I've never dreamt of being a maid. I wanted to be a psychologist. But dreams don't come true for people like me.

I was walking fast to keep step with her. The airport was packed with people. I didn't want to get lost. I had no phone at that time.

Suddenly, she turned and pushed me in a very brusque manner yelling, "Stay back, you peasant! One metre behind me! You are not on my level. You are a servant. Do you understand that?!"

The child startled in my arms. People stopped to assist at the scene. Her friend looked down. I froze. 'This can be happening. It's a nightmare. It can't be true. Slavery was abolished many years ago. I am not a slave. There are no slaves.'

I believed I didn't breathe for many minutes from the shock. My chest hurt. My heart was bleeding. In disbelief, I stayed behind trying to accept the fact that I was indeed a slave of the 20th century.

In the aeroplane, the blue blood descendent went to the first class. The two children and I were guided to a few chairs back, the second class. I couldn't believe she left the children with me.

I sat and put them both on my lap hiding my face behind them. I allowed my tears to roll down thousands and I prayed with selfishness and devotion. 'Your mother is a despicable creature. I am so sorry for you both. Forgive me if I pray for this plane to crash. I believe that you would be better off in heaven than with her.'

I prayed like never before. There was no hope for me. No future and no kindness. There was no place in this world for a purposeless person like me. It was so dark that I couldn't see my spirit. 'God, please, if you exist, make this plane crash. Take me away from here. Have mercy on my soul.'

God was busy.

We've got to Rome alive. Her mother came to give us a lift. I was afraid to look into her eyes. My boss was a monster, in my mind her mother must have been worse. I was wrong. Her mother was kind, like all the other family members I met.

"My daughter is ill," she confessed to me. "Please don't go away too. These children need you."

So they knew she was crazy. Yet, they left the children with her. I couldn't comprehend why.

"These children are in mortal danger with her. She's out of control," I said in a broken Italian.

"We know. Her husband is doing his best to keep them safe."

"If she snaps, they are dead. She's a ticking bomb," I insisted.

"She must take her medication. My son-in-law is making sure that she does."

"He's away with work the whole day. Anything could happen in that time. Put her in a hospital!" 'A loony bin. In a straightjacket. She's crazy dangerous,' I thought in my mind.

"She'd die in there. She'd kill herself. We've tried. She needs her children."

The sacrifice of the lambs.

Dinner was ready. Her family invited me to sit with them. I wasn't hungry, but I sat because they insisted. My boss was upstairs. When she arrived in the dining room and saw me at the table, she lost it. She walked towards me like a hungry lion, grabbed my hand and pulled me up from the chair.

"You are a servant. Your place is with the servants. In the kitchen, peasant. Now!"

Some of her family members got up from the chairs and tried to persuade her to let go of me. The monster was deaf and furious.

"Let the girl eat. She didn't do anything wrong," they said.

"This philistine doesn't even speak Italian. She's stupider than a bucket."

"She moved to Italy two weeks ago. This is not her language. Give her some time to learn."

"Who, her? A peasant learning Italian? Impossible!"

They had to stand down as she was inflexible.

The lady pushed me with rage in the kitchen and locked the door twice. I stood there petrified like a marble statue for... I don't know. Then I felt like I was going to faint. I looked around for something to sit on. Or a wall to lean against. There was either of these two things. The room was small, it contained only kitchen appliances on both sides. I could have leant against the door but what if someone would have wanted to get in? The door opened in the kitchen, not in the dining room.

So I made a step to the right on the corridor between the appliances, which was less than one metre wide, and sat on the black granite pavement. I leant my back against the oven and... froze again. My mind was empty, I couldn't feel a thing. No pain, no despair, no rage, nothing. Just emptiness.

I don't know how long it passed until the door opened, and someone pushed the baby girl in. She walked towards me and reached her hands to me. I got up and took her in my arms. She looked sleepy, probably just woke up from the nap I put her to when we've got there.

She wanted to play, so she started to open the cupboards. When she saw a bag of her favourite biscuits, she asked for one. I opened it and give it to her. She took it and put it in my mouth. It was then when I realised that ten days have passed since I ate something. The whole time I was living with the blue blood monster. I chewed the biscuit absently, it had a lot of chocolate on top. I will always remember its square form, but not the taste.

Our permanence at the villa – or castle as they called it – lasted for three days. Her family excused her poor behaviour again. They also begged me not to leave like the other girl. And the previous one, and the other one and again. It turned out that no girl could resist longer than a week with that evil creature. In fact, the girl I met only remained for a month. She moved to Italy three months before, as she told me, but she worked for them for less than a month before she resigned. Because the girl signed a contract, she needed to wait for a substitute. I came at the right moment.

I didn't even try explaining once more what was at stake. They knew she was not fit to be a mother. They condemned the two children to a life in constant danger. It was not my place to make them aware of the huge mistake they were making. They were smart… but the name… the reputation was more important than the lives of those two innocent creatures.

On our way back, I've made up my mind, 'If the plane doesn't crash, I am leaving. I will call my sponsor and tell him the truth. He will help me. I know he likes me. I am a woman, I felt it. He will take me away from this crazy monster. I am going back to my country. I will be a farmer. It's nothing wrong with working the land. It's an honest living. I will raise chickens, pigs, and ducks. And I will marry the boyfriend I left when I came here. This is my destiny. I've tried to change something already written in my book's life. I was ungrateful and irrational. I should have never left. Enough with dreaming big. I can't be what I crave to be. You can't fight against destiny.'

So I did. He came right away. It was 9pm when he asked permission from the monster to take me to the beach close by.

In tears, I told him everything. I told him that the last meal I had was at his place before I moved there. I told him that she thinks that slavery is legal. And I told him that those children were in danger and there was nothing anyone could do for them.

He hugged me and that night on the beach he promised to never allow anyone to treat me that way again.

The next day in the late afternoon, while she was resting, I gathered my things. Then I went to her and told her that I couldn't remain a day more in that house, "I will not sign the contract you are preparing."

At first, she thought it was a joke, and she laughed with cruelty, "Don't be ridiculous! Where are you planning on going? You have no one here."

"I am going home."

She looked at me with so much hate in her yellow eyes and bellowed unwritable words. I stood on the door and endured the murderous rage she unleashed upon me. She whipped me countless offences. For almost one hour, she washed the floor with my dignity and deprived me of humanity.

I didn't blink. I checked the clock. My sponsor was going to be there in 15 minutes. 'She has more than enough time to murder me even more than once,' I thought. 'She wouldn't even be prosecuted for it. She is insane.' But I didn't care.

When I took the decision to go to Italy, I knew I was going to die in there. Except that I pictured myself being shot with a Colt or a Smith by a short gangster while eating ice cream in a pastry shop.

But when you're dead, you're dead. It doesn't really matter who killed you and why.

Someone rang the door, I knew it was my sponsor. I turned around intended to open it. She ordered me to step aside, "Don't touch that door. Don't touch anything in this house again!"

I went to my room in the basement to take my suitcase. Someone knocked on the door.

"Come in," I murmured.

It was the husband.

"I am truly sorry you are leaving, but I understand," he said. "You don't deserve to be treated this way. Please, accept my apologies. She is in not in herself in the last period."

I wondered if she's ever been a good person. I doubted it very much. "Your wife needs professional help. But you already know that. Just... just keep the children safe."

"Thank you for everything and good luck," he replied while reaching his right hand to me.

I shook it, took my black suitcase, and left the mouldy room.

The beast and my sponsor were standing on the door. They finished talking. He looked at me and smiled with sadness. That was the second time since I was in that house when I felt the tears fighting to get out. I held them back. I didn't want her to see me crying.

I passed next to her holding my breath. I thought she was going to hit me. I feared she had a knife in her hands. In fact, I was convinced that she kept one with her at all times. Or a gun. In my mind, she was a cold-blooded criminal hiding under a mask of insanity. She was worse than a gangster. She had no rules and no one to answer to.

I closed my eyes when she bent to take something from the floor. I went outside and got into the car with my heart racing. I thought it was going to get out of my chest. My sponsor started the engine immediately. She ran after the car and threw the slippers she brought me the second day I was there, "Take these dirty slippers with you. It's the only thing you're going to have from me, philistine!"

"This woman is crazy!" he said with anguish. "I've never seen anything like this before."

I sighed with relief and let the tears fall. The nightmare was over. I was safe and very, very hungry.

From the frying pan into the fire

We had a walk on the beach in the moonlight. He hugged me while I cried until I had no more tears. Then he promised again to keep me safe, "You will smile again, beautiful girl. You will smile."

I believed him.

These words are impressed in my memory for eternity. It feels like it was yesterday.

He took me to his place where he lived with his mother. I don't know what she told her. I wasn't supposed to be there. How he explained my presence there, is a mystery.

We didn't speak of love. Not that night at least. We didn't kiss, and we most certainly didn't make love. He was responsible for me, and he was doing his best to protect me. But I knew it was more than that, he fancied me as much as I fancied him.

A few weeks have passed, six or seven. I bonded with his mother a lot. We worked together on the small crop they had. I helped her cooking and cleaning. We've made pickles and donated the jars to charities. We fundraised and met with friends. She loved her son very much. She was incessantly speaking about him. I was amazed by how close they were. A man in his forties, unmarried, living with his elderly mother was pretty uncommon in my country.

One day he took me with him in the morning and checked me in a hostel until he finished work. Then we went on a weekend holiday. *Forni di Sopra*, a touristic village in the mountains. His mother called him every ten minutes. I found it odd.

The first night, after dinner, we had our first intercourse. I was almost 25. It didn't hurt as I heard was supposed to, and it lasted less than 30 seconds.

He pushed me aside and shouted, "You've lied to me. You are not a virgin!"

I felt humiliated, offended, and confused. "What makes you say that? I swear to God, no man has ever touched me before."

"Liar!" he yelled again. "You didn't bleed at all."

I touched myself. He was right, there was no blood. That wasn't normal. All virgins bleed a lot the first time. I read it in a book, *The Borgias*. I thought something was very wrong with my body and I plead for clemency. In my knees, with tear-stained face, I swore on my life that I was pure and chaste before that night.

He didn't believe me and the sky crashed over my head. 'Nobody gives a damn on me. My word has no weight. I am a human of inferior. What am I going to do? Is there anything I can do to fix this?' I found no answer.

The next day in the morning we went back. He was changed. I did my best to convince him of my innocence. He sweetened a bit before we reached his house.

On Sunday we went to visit a museum. His mother came with us. I was happy that he seemed to like me again. We hid like children after a ladder in a corridor, and we kissed. Probably for the first time.

That evening, after dinner, he told his mother that we were in love. She didn't see that coming. Her attitude towards me changed in a heartbeat. Suddenly, I wasn't protégé of her friend, the priest, anymore. I was a thief. A thief of her son's heart. A thief of her only reason to live.

She wasn't happy sharing her time with me any longer. She stopped inviting me to visit her friends with her. She didn't like me to cook dinner for her son. She found something to complain every second.

My tone of voice scratched her hearing.

My uncertain Italian become insufferable for her.

My laughter was annoying.

My love for order and cleanliness got on her nerves.

She snapped every time I asked a question or had an idea.

My smile disappeared slowly. There was winter in my heart.

Oblivious to his mother conduct, at the end of October of that year – 2000 – her son decided to take me to Romania to ask for my hand from my parents. At least that was what he told me. In reality, he wanted to visit something close to his heart.

But I won't be mentioning what to avoid litigation and belittle a fantastic charitable project he's been working on for years when I met him.

My father didn't like him at all. Nevertheless, he gave his blessing. On the second night he was in Romania, he told me that the next day we were expected somewhere I don't remember. I snapped, and I raised my voice, "You never discuss anything me. You never ask for my opinion. What if I don't want to go? What if I have different plans? You just give orders. I am a human being, not a puppet, you know?"

"How dare you to raise the voice at me? I have a university degree! *You*...? You are..." ... *a peasant* I guessed he wanted to say.

That night I saw the history repeating itself. I got off the car and slammed the door. He left, and I didn't see or heard from him for two days. Then he came, and we discussed and planned a few trips with my nephews and nieces. We had a lot of fun, and the offence was forgotten.

We went back to Italy, and the days passed as before. We never slept in the same room. If wasn't appropriate. And we never had sex after that first night in the mountains.

A Saturday afternoon, after lunch, his mother went to have her regular nap – siesta. My fiancé asked me to go with him to his room to watch a movie. And I went. We lay in bed under the duvet when the door opened, and his mother got in.

His mother and I both were outraged. She, because I was in her son's bed. I, because she didn't care to knock. We were not doing anything because he showed no interest in penetrating me while I was still confused about my strange body reaction. But her mother didn't know that. As I said, for her mother, I was a robber.

She cursed and accused me of decadence. Her son got upset and demanded peace and quiet while sending his mother away.

The incident was immediately forgotten by my soon to be husband. But not by his mother. From that moment on, she locked me in my room every night I went to bed. Her behaviour became more and more aggressive and rude.

One evening, after dinner, I was having a bath when I heard her complaining about me to her son. I was hurt and shocked, but I said nothing to anyone. I thought it was a singular event. Maybe I've done something I didn't realise.

Then I heard her doing the same the next evening, and the other and another one. All in the same context, which was while having a bath. I decided to avoid finding myself in the bathroom after dinner as that seemed to be the moment when she spoke with her son.

The days went by all the same. He went to work, I remained with his mother. I found myself countless things to do. The house in decay was huge, three levels. More of a block of apartments or a castle. There was such a mess everywhere. Disorder, clutter, dust, spider webs reigned everywhere, especially on the floors where nobody went. It reminded me of *Great Expectations*, the house of Miss Havisham. I asked for permission to take care of that. She granted it. We both were eager to stay as apart as possible.

Every morning, until December, after her son went to work she came and unlocked my door. I had breakfast and went upstairs. I uncluttered and polished every surface in every room. If before only the ground floor was habitable and three bedrooms on the second floor, by December of 2000, three more beautiful bedrooms flourished.

We kept having lunch together, I really don't know why. We weren't friends anymore, we were rivals. She couldn't stand the sight of me, and it hurt so, so badly. I didn't try to make her o like me. I didn't like her either. I was upset with her. Her behaviour and attachment to her son nauseated me. It didn't seem normal. Not to me at least.

She lived only for her son. I sometimes felt sorry for her because she was so lonely and teary. My future mother-in-law missed her husband who died a few years back. She used to go to the cemetery almost every day.

She told me her love story at the beginning of our acquaintance. I cringed in horror because everything I gathered was... a story of obedience. Her husband ordered, and she followed. It wasn't a tale of love and passion as we intend it. She did things for him, and he brought home the pay. Nevertheless, she loved him dearly. She tried to teach me that one day.

"If your husband buys you a cloth and tells you is a dress, you wear that cloth every day to demonstrate your love for him."

I was outraged and replied without thinking, "If my husband loves me, he would never buy me a cloth."

She didn't like my statement. In fact, I have the suspect that was when she stopped liking me. I was too arrogant.

One evening, my fiancé offered to teach me to use the computer. He took me into his office and explained how it worked. My birthday was near, I was turning 25, it was like a gift in advance. I still remember how complicated sounded everything.

The mouse was moving on the screen in a very erratic manner.

"Stop it," he chuckled.

"It isn't me moving it. It's possessed. How do you manage to keep it steady? How do you manage to click on something? It's impossible to make it listen to your commands."

He showed me and seemed so easy for him. I put both hands on that bloody mouse, and it still moved randomly.

But I wanted to learn, and from that day on, every time she had her afternoon nap, I went into her son office and tamed the mouse to follow my precise directions.

She complained to her son about that. I was learning things I didn't need to know. He prohibited me from going in his office in his absence and especially not to touch the computer. I was allowed to clean though.

I cried and didn't understand why they wanted me to be ignorant.

Were they communists too?

To soothe me, he taught me to play chess.

Three days later I beat him three times in a row. He never played chess with me again. He preferred to have the computer as an adversary. I learnt not to beat anyone in any game. Ever.

One evening during dinner, they were gossiping about some Romanian friends they had.

"Mama," he said, "do you remember Radu?"

She nodded yes.

"He had an incident and destroyed the car. I told him not to buy a car. He came here to work not to buy cars."

My heart was bleeding. It was exactly the same thing the countess told me, "You didn't come here to learn the language, you came here to work."

I reproached both and accused them of chauvinism, "Romanians are humans too. Why wouldn't they have the right to buy a car if they had the money? How can you be friends with someone and speak badly of them on their back?"

"Shut your mouth!" he howled. "You don't know what you're talking about."

But I knew what I was talking about. I knew his friend too. He renovated an apartment building my fiancé owned on the beach. The man I loved paid my fellow Romanian with his friendship. No money was ever involved. My husband-to-be was an important person, he had connections. His friendship was a huge investment. He thought that too as he also held true to feeling happiness when a Romanian friend has a car accident.

Another time while watching TV they were criticising a journalist for her ideas. As I was sharing the same thought, I dared to partner with them.

"Who are you to judge?" my future husband-to-be asked with disdain.

I froze for a few seconds then I murmured, "But you just said that too. Both of you. I agree with you, that's why I spoke."

"Well, you don't have this right. We are born in this country, same as her. You are a guest in this land. Respect it and its people."

Her mother acknowledged and approved of her son's attitude and comments, of course.

Then he prohibited me from using the verb *want* at present tense. "You are only allowed to say *I would like to*. There is no *I want* for you. – *L'erba voglio non cresce nemmeno nel giardino del re*."

At that time I found it utterly humiliating. Now I know that children are taught manners when they scream, "I want." Although, in my opinion, that is not present tense, that is imperative mood. Italian was not my mother tongue, I was learning it. And they failed to explain the difference. They only ordered and demanded obedience without question.

Communism much? Slavery? Xenophobia?

The quirkiest part of this story is that I knew I was about to get married, but he never asked me. He, or they, decided when and where the wedding will be held and who was going to ask us the vows. But I was never consulted.

One day he told me that it was time for me to look for a job and he found me a cleaner role. That day I knew it was time for me to leave, but believe it or not, I loved him.

Two days before Christmas they had a special guest. The priest who was going to give us his blessing while my future husband-to-be put the engagement ring on my finger. I really don't know when was that due to happen, if it was Christmas day or Eve.

We were already engaged in *words*, but he never asked me if I wanted to get married. As he didn't ask me if I wanted to have an engagement gathering. I don't know with whom he consulted with. By logic, it was the priest and his mother. I was merely a spectator.

My fiancé offered his bedroom to the priest. I found that to be a wonderful gesture. His room was the biggest and the prettiest. My fiancé cared for the priest. I liked that. I was supposed to care for that priest too. I should have cared because he was the one that helped me get to Italy and meet my future husband.

The next morning, on the 24th, Christmas Eve, I asked my future husband-to-be where did he sleep the night before.

"In my mother's room," he replied.

After a second of confusion where in my mind I imagined different scenarios, I said, "I didn't know were two beds in her room."

"There is only one."

That statement hit me in the crown of the head like a baseball bat. I needed to make sure it wasn't a misinterpretation, "Are you telling me that you slept in the same bed with your mother when there are at least three other free bedrooms in this house? How could you? What is wrong with you, people? My brother was five when he refused to sleep in the same bed with my mother. You are thirty-eight!" (Probably. I can't remember. To be honest, I've never known his age.)

"How dare you?! How dare you to judge us? It's none of your business. You have no right. The priest was not scandalised, but you are? You're pathetic."

I was disgusted and perturbed. That wasn't normal behaviour in my mind.

He felt the same for me.

That day I understood what my future will be like if I stayed. I told him that I can't marry him. I told him that I wanted to leave as I couldn't accept that. "It's too much."

I heard him discussing with the priest. The engagement was off, but not because I refused, but because both decided I was not the right wife for him.

"She's insolent, crude, and disobedient. She doesn't get along with my mother who is always in distress. I have second thoughts, father. Forgive me, but I won't propose to her as we agreed. She needs to be educated and shaped. Let's postpone this, shall we?"

The priest's words broke my heart and the trust in the men of God. He didn't only agree with him and his mother – who was present, but added more. He was disappointed in me and asked for humble forgiveness from both his hosts.

Many serious allegations were made. I heard them clearly then. I know I have, but I don't know in which context. Probably the walls were thin, and they were not aware of that as they've never had guests who spoke in the house while they were in their quarters.

I don't remember the words because the shock was planetary and the pain was unbearable. I imposed myself to forget and, with the years, I learnt to forgive.

To the day, the priest and the nun retain me responsible for a good family distress.

To the day I am the only culprit in this appalling story.

To the day, neither of them, the nun and the priest, speak to me.

I made an appeal to their understanding. I told them that I was treated worse than an animal. I cried and sworn it was the honest truth. They didn't even conceive it was possible. They looked at me in pain and took the distances. The word of a highly educated Italian against the word of a Romanian farmer. It was obvious who was going to win. They thought I was a deranged person. I thought… they wanted to be blind on purpose. The people who took me to Italy needed support. And what a better alliance than a marriage? The creature I loved, was a powerful man with loads of connections.

The priest used to say that the encounter between my sponsor and I was divine intervention. He merely assisted to it. I thought that too... before he accused me with forgery and before I found out what they all thought of me. I was chosen because I was a beautiful *peasant*. They trusted I would be a mute slave with no human desires for all my life.

They expected me to move like a pawn when they ordered. They put me in chains again. They didn't know that I had dreams and hopes. But mostly, they ignored that I wanted to live among normal people in an ambient of respect and consideration.

I left as I said I would. The date of the wedding was set. I never knew it. He was livid when I finally told him I preferred to be a cleaner for all my life than a *queen* in a cage. It was an incredible offence. Everybody knew he was getting married. His reputation was going to suffer. I really didn't care at that time. I just wanted to be free.

I lived in that house for eight months. The discussions I witnessed to by mistake or because they didn't consider my presence, were appalling. The way they spoke about everybody, the critics and the judgements were worthy of a god. No one was better than them. No one deserved to be alive. No one deserved to be helped. They were the only righteous people.

They were wolfs in sheep's clothing. But the monster was me because I refused to wear the cloth my fiancé bought for me.

I am aware of the fact they have a different version of this story. He told it to my sister, and he told it to the priest. He wasn't a racist. He didn't disconsider me because I was a Romanian farmer with no university degree. He discondered me because I wasn't docile. In his mind, he was an incredibly generous person, and I should have kissed the earth he stepped on. I was expected to act like a dog. Unfortunately, I had the gift of speech.

Isn't this what humans do? Our truth is the only truth that matters? Are we really incapable of objectivity?

I think we don't want to be objective because we are too self-centred, and we lack compassion and empathy.

It is impossible to realise how much harm we do when we are convinced of being great human beings.

It took me several years to move on. I had periods of utter despair because, as I said, I really loved the wolf. I looked up to him. As I did with Ceausescu.

After that I went from bad to worse over and over and over again. Every time I thought, 'It can't get worse than this. It's not humanly possible. God won't allow it. He created me too.'

But God was too busy with wars and cataclysms. Too many needed to be saved. He gave me the will to keep it together and fight for my life.

But I was so weary, lonely and hopeless. I really needed His divine intervention.

Before leaving my homeland, I was convinced that if you work hard and mind your own business people will treat you with respect. But that was a fantasy. In reality, for ten years I have been abused in countless ways.

My nationality defined and closed all the doors in front of me. Men expected and demanded me to open my legs though. My refusal brought me a lot more hate and disdain that I could ever imagine.

My reliability, honesty, commitment and so on were never considered.

After I got very ill, I went to therapy. Even my counsellor discriminated me. She told me to go home and be a farmer if I couldn't handle to live in the modern world. I paid an arm and a leg to be humiliated and belittled.

Hate, disdain, abuse, and lack of humanity are evidence of modernism and emancipation.

How sad is that?

Bosses in my workplaces exploited me to exhaustion disparaging all my efforts. And if that was not enough they abused and tortured me emotionally and physically.

I had no one to turn to. I didn't even dream to press charges. Only the thought of speaking with the police terrified me. I knew they would blame me as I saw it happening so many times in movies. The victims pay for what the perpetrators have done on to them.

I went to bed crying every night and became more and more despondent. I had to force myself to get out of bed. People like me don't have the right to feel depressed. In the end, I was living in a modern country. I had a job. What else did I need?

At some point, I was terrified to get out of the house. Then, eventually, I got very ill.

Doctors in the hospital accused me of taking advantage of their system. A few refused to visit me, but they sent me the bill to pay. And I paid as I did with everything that was given to me. I had nothing for free. Not that I asked or expected it, of course. I didn't leave my country to ask for charity from another one. I went there to have a future. And I paid with my life.

Ten years later, I couldn't take any more. I was a dead man walking. So I went home to lick my wounds.

Many other appalling things happened to me in the country of Leonardo da Vinci. *Ten Years in Italy,*

Three Weeks a Human describes some of them in detail. Read it.

And if you like, check out Humans Cursed by Geography in the Pursuit of Happiness. This book gathers the two memoirs set in Romania and Italy – *Oranges at Christmas in a Communist Country* and *Ten Years in Italy, Three Weeks a Human*.

Great Expectations, Charity & Condescension

In 2014, Gene, a British friend, helped me to move to England. I fell in love with this country right away. I adore the rain, the green, the politeness of people....

Despite all that, I had a really hard time to get used to the new reality. I have lived in Italy before, the modern world, but England is a different... planet.

Gene gave me shelter and fed me chocolate because that was the only thing I could eat. Then she pushed me to believe I was a great human being who deserved a decent future.

I owe her my life.

But the truth is I didn't want to leave my homeland. Not ever. I am very attached to my roots and many other small things that many disconsider. I didn't want to leave my parents and my home. But I had to because there was nothing to do in my country. I was heartbroken.

After the communism, Romania went from bad to worse. Everything was new... but old. If you know what I mean.

I had so many hopes. I thought my country will be accepted in the world and opportunities will be open to every fellow national who wanted to do something different with their lives.

With every new political party at the power, one by one, all my dreams were broken.

After Italy, and after I saw my country sinking lower and lower than in all my nightmares, my hopes reduced to dust.

I was a human wreck. I knew I was a good human being and I deserved to have the opportunity to do what I wanted in my life. But everybody made me understood that I was merely a slave with no rights, just duties.

I sacrificed everything to help my parents while pursuing my childhood dream unconsciously.

Because my self-confidence was null, I couldn't dare to think that I am allowed to become a writer. I knew that was my purpose, but maybe not in this life. Maybe in the next.

At some point, breathing became a huge burden. I didn't belong in this world. Nobody recognised me as a human being. I came to life too soon or too early. It was not my time.

I moved to England to get out from emotional lethargy and to find something to do. Anything really.

Learning English was another hidden dream. So I thought that I could clean apartments while studying.

I went to an employment agency, and in two days I found my first job. I needed tax papers, of course.

The agency offered me five hours of work a day. I told them that I needed money right away and a full-time job. They promised that I will have those hours.

I walked to work and back which more than 16 miles a day because I couldn't afford to buy a ticket bus. Not that I wanted one. I needed to learn the surroundings, and I had plenty of time.

A week later, I was working maybe eight hours a week in total.

I was shy, afraid and had no self-confidence. I didn't know that I could leave them any minute if someone else offered me the employment I desired. In fact, I was called several times but I didn't find the courage to accept to the detriment of the agency I was working for.

But two weeks later they still didn't keep their promise, so I told them that I can't go on like this and I was leaving. They offered me a full-time job in a warehouse immediately. They had that job all the time, but I was a too good cleaner, too reliable, too honest. When I threatened to leave they did their best to keep me.

In the meanwhile, Gene managed to force me to apply for an office job. I laughed ironically convinced she was insane.

In Italy, I have followed evening courses and

worked in administration for five years. I was more than qualified, but my English was very poor.

The worst part was that I had no self-esteem. I didn't think I deserved it. It took her a lot of time to convince. She wrote my CV sent it over to the company and one day, I got a call from them telling me to go for an interview.

Long story short, I was offered the job. But I was not okay with leaving the other job because I committed. In my mind, it was not correct behaviour. Gene told me it was absolutely fine. So I gathered all the courage that I didn't have and resigned from the other job.

They asked me what another job I was offered.

"Call analyst," I said.

"What job is that?"

"Office job."

The woman looked at me and laughed. She didn't believe me. The look in her eyes was very eloquent, "You are a blue-collar, not a white one."

I couldn't blame her, I thought that myself.

"Come back to us if that doesn't work for you. We'll take you back with opened arms."

I didn't like the tone she used. Contempt is

something I cannot stand. All my life I have been treated with condescension. I promised to never go back to work for her again.

Three years later, I am still working as a call analyst for three days a week and writing for the other four.

If that agency employee would see me now, she would still not respect me. If I told her that I am an author she would laugh again. Even if I showed her my books, it would be in vain. I am not worthy of her consideration. For her, everything I am good at is slogging for people like her.

Do you know why?

Because of my origins. I am a human of inferior birth.

The worst part in this is that she was an immigrant too. But she was blessed by geography as her passport had "Australia" on it.

However, I am sure she is not a chauvinist only with me. A creature like her discriminates every human on this earth who was born in the wrong country.

Since I left Romania, I have seen and experienced

countless behaviours like this. My origins defined me. Like every immigrant is a bad person.

But are they really?

Is England a country without native criminals? What about the USA? Italy? France?

No. But it's so easy to see the faults in others than in yourself. Isn't it?

You might have not noticed, but often a person changes the tone of voice when they speak with an immigrant. I am sure they don't do that on purpose nor that they are aware of that. It comes naturally. Most of the time without malice I want to believe.

In the work environments, often the foreign are discondered by default when a higher position comes up. Their work is belittled. As a whole, we are all fantastic, but individually, an immigrant is just *good*. Not always, of course. And not in every company.

I have never wanted to have a leading position. I never applied for one, so I can't speak from experience. My friends are complaining, and I am sorry for them.

You might think I am paranoid. I would think that too if I didn't know any better. I am more sensitive, of course. As I am more sensitive to beauty and kindness.

You try being an immigrant and you'll see. But if your nationality is not one of the third worlds, you will not be treated like me. Therefore, I cannot prove to you that I am right to feel what I feel. Unfortunately, or fortunately.

I learnt to ignore it and give the benefit of the doubt. Not for them, but for me.

I cannot waste one second of my time to feel discriminated and humiliated. I am too busy pursuing my dream. It doesn't matter what a person does or says to me now. Nothing affects me anymore because I worked on my mind every single minute of these three years.

I have forced it to believe that I am a human being like everybody else.

But it took me more than ten years to get here. I had to write down phrases like the following ones and read them out loud every single day of my life since I left Italy (2010).

I am a good person;

I deserve to be respected;

I am a human being, nothing less and nothing more;

I am worthy of consideration;

I have the right to dream;

I am very good at my job;

And so on.

Even now, I walk for four miles every morning when I go to work and repeat these phrases over and over and over again. I do the same when I come back.

Did you have to do that to think you're human?

I don't think so.

I have been fighting for all my life since I was born to prove that I am worthy of being considered a human being.

If you read *Humans Cursed by Geography in the Pursuit of Happiness*, you will understand why I have to do this.

I've always been a very timid person. I knew I was a good human, but people led me to believe I was unworthy. Every single day of my life someone did or said something awful to me. My life in Italy was an endless nightmare. I fought so badly to keep functioning.

I knew I didn't deserve to be treated that way and that made me feel even worse.

For thirty-nine years I lived in constant fear, and I trembled like a leaf in the wind. Literally. I couldn't paint my nails or put eyeliner and mascara on because of that.

Five years after I moved to Italy, my hands started to shake so badly that I couldn't carry a tray with glasses or mugs filled with liquids. I was a waitress at that time. It was embarrassing, and the efforts I had to put up to avoid the spilling was inhuman. It was my job to serve coffee and drinks, and I had to do until it became impossible to get out of bed. But I had to go to work. I've never missed a day. Ever. And I was so ill and so weary.

I kept working, of course, and I get worse and worse. I used to go to bed crying in despair, I couldn't sleep, I couldn't eat.

I was afraid of people.

I was afraid to open my mouth.

I was terrified to raise my head and look into their eyes.

When I turned forty (in 2015), I made an ultimate promise to myself. I was to work night and day to build up confidence and self-esteem. I have tried to work on that for many years before, of course, I said it above. But I failed miserably.

This time, failing was not an option. But this is written in a different book yet to be published.

If you didn't read *It's Never Game Over,* it is time to remediate to learn what else I do every day to take my life into my own hands.

When people look at me today, they see a very confident person. Many are very intimidated by me.

The truth is I still tremble inside. My hands are still unsteady when I put mascara on. I still cannot paint my nails.

I don't go out because I still fear people.

I am still reticent to speak because my uncertain English pronunciation gets worse when somebody makes me feel inferior – on purpose or not.

My face turns beet red and my pulse accelerates if someone addresses me. I wish I was invisible. I wish I lived in a forest.

Despite all that, I dress up elegantly. People are convinced that I do it for vanity or to be admired. I don't care what people say or think of me as long as they don't mistreat or try to kill me. I care what I think of me. Because it's with me that I live for 24 hours a day. I dress this way to make my mind understand that I am human worthy of respect. It's one of the ways I work on my self-esteem. I have improved tremendously since I am living in England. But I am still billions of miles away from feeling uncomfortable in my human shell.

When I know that I look amazing, I tremble even harder. Like I didn't have the right to wear those clothes or to look like that.

I love my day job very much.

Do you know why?

Because it's a solitary one. I am alone with my headphones. I don't have to open my mouth too often. I don't have to watch people in the eyes.

Nobody can hurt me when I am at work. I feel very grateful for it. One day I will forget to speak.

Nobody knows, nobody even imagines what's in my heart. For them, I am a normal individual. But there is nothing normal about me. I know that a different person in my place would be dead by now. But I am still here, fighting the invisible foe.

I have a dream and a purpose, and this is my last battle. I am going to win. I have to.

***

When I told my friends that I am going to be a worldwide known author, at first, they thought I was joking.

Then they called me crazy.

Later on, they told me to give up because it was too hard.

When I didn't, they made me understand that I was delusional.

And these are people who care for me. And I know they do.

I tried to explain to them that it was not a caprice. Vanity is not something I understand. But they couldn't see it. For them, I am a Romanian farmer, not a writer. They couldn't see what I force myself to see.

They discriminated me without intention. My friends. People like me. The only difference between them and me is the country of origin.

Only the other day I was confessing that I am investing all my savings in publishing my work and nothing comes back from this.

"Give up then! What are you waiting for? You've tried."

No. There is no try for me, there is only win. But who can understand that?

Can I even blame them for this?

No. I can't, and I won't. I don't have time for that.

This is my battle. I am alone against the unbeatable destiny. All I want is to be allowed to fight for my life. I don't need discouragements. I am not a child anymore, and the worst part is that I have never lived.

Read my new release: _Author for Life or for a Living?_

Cristina G.

When the Brexit Referendum had the notorious outcome, my shock was planetary.

I didn't know what English people thought about the immigrants till that day.

You see, I don't watch TV, listen to the radio or read newspapers, and so on. I live under a bell utterly unaware of what's happening around me.

It's an extreme measure in order to hold on to my life. I really can't cope with so much free hate, and pain broadcasted every second. I am trying to survive, and the only way I can do it is to protect myself from external negativity.

I decide what to watch and when. Usually are only motivational and inspirational true stories.

The Brexit Referendum slapped me in the face. I watched people crying and twisting, fearing for their future and lives.

Is it true that English people voted Leave because they hate those like me?

I pay taxes and work hard every day. I don't ask for any charity. I don't steal, and I don't cheat. I am respectful of the law, things and every living being. I never broke a rule.

Why would anyone hate me?

Only because my passport states that I am Romanian? But I am human before being Romanian. I am a very good human.

Why would you want to send me home?

What have I done to you or to this country?

I don't even have a GP. I never went to a hospital. I buy my painkillers in supermarkets.

I was despondent for a while. But I don't have time for sadness. I have to work on my dream. It is now or never. If they want me out, I will leave. The loss is not mine.

For now, I am grateful for this opportunity, and I will never resent this country for the decision to vote Leave. It's their right.

My hands are frozen because I can't afford to pay my electrical bill. I invest everything in my dream. Money, time, body, and soul. I don't know for how long I'll be here, so every minute spent detesting, regretting and crying over the past, it's a lost one.

Plus, I am providing for the care of my octogenarian parents whom I miss immensely. It is for them too that I work so hard. I would like to repay them for so many sacrifices they had to do to raise ten children during an oppressive communist regime.

I believe that whatever you give, you will receive. Maybe not now or in this life, but it will come back to you.

So I choose to spread the love and mind my own business. Always and regardless.

If you discriminate, consciously or unconsciously, you risk your future.

What if in a next life you will be the immigrant?

What if in twenty years from now, my country will rise to the top and yours will go to the bottom?

When you give your opinion think of why you have that opinion in the first place.

Is it fair to discriminate a whole country because of the mishaps of a few?

Is it fair to slap a child across their face because they have darker skin?

Is it fair to expect your wife to be a slave instead of a partner?

Is it fair to blame the immigrants for the issues your country faces?

Look around you. Look inside you. Then look at me. What is the difference between you and me? What gives the right to look down to me?

And when I say *me*, I am referring to *every immigrant* in this world.

I am responsible for my own actions only.

"One should treat others as one would like others to treat oneself." Isn't that correct?

What's the purpose of writing Great Charters if nobody respects what's in them?

Open your heart human and see the love in my eyes. I don't want to take anything from you. I want what's mine by birthright. I want to be considered human just like you.

Please, don't cry papa

I have been treated in diverse ways during these years, but seldom fairly.

For many, too many, I am a human of inferior birth. Not worthy of consideration.

I have no motherland now. No identity. I can barely remember the streets of the village I have lived in for twenty-four years of my life.

I feel like I don't belong anywhere.

I feel like the world doesn't want me.

I haven't seen my eight (remaining) siblings all together in seventeen years. I know that only a tragedy will reunite us. But I don't want that tragedy. I want to hug my siblings and have lunch with them. And I want to visit my dearest's brother tomb and leave a flower on it to make him realise we haven't forgotten him. He will live forever in our hearts.

I've sacrificed my entire life for my dearest ones.

I bought the cheapest products, I never had a holiday, I didn't go out for meals, and I didn't switch the heat on in the winter to be able to save some money and send them home.

My octogenarian parents pray for my siblings and me every day. It breaks my heart to see the tears on their wrinkled faces every time I speak to them from behind a monitor.

"When are you coming home, my child?"

"I don't know, papa. I can't afford it just yet. Please don't cry."

But he can't help himself. And I cry with him cursing my destiny.

My father used to be such a strong man. He worked night and day to provide for my nine siblings and me. He used to get up at 2 in the morning and walked for 15 + 15 km in the snow to go to work. He was never ill. He never said that the snow was too high and didn't find a transportation method.

He never missed a single day of work. I learnt that from him. Reliability and sacrifice are what I do best.

For whole these years I fell asleep with the terror that I will never see my parents and my siblings alive.

Do you know how that feels? What that does to your moral?

The UK, the country I love very much, has voted "Leave."
- *Should I pack my bags?*
- *Should I give up my dream?*
- *Nobody wants Romanians. Is there anywhere I could go?*
- *How am I going to provide for my octogenarian parents who survived the Second World War and raised ten children under an oppressive communist regime?*
- *Is it really true that this world is not for people like me?*
- *What should I do?*
- *What can I do?*
- *What would You do if you were me?*
- *Would you dare to ask for your human rights?*

- *Would you cry and feel alone in the whole universe?*

I hope you'll never have to find out.

As for you, brothers and sisters who twist in despair and miss your roots, do not lose hope. Keep fighting, keep loving humans. We are not all the same.

You will find a way. You are not alone.

I know I am one of the lucky ones. I didn't cross oceans and seas in shipwrecks. I didn't walk for thousands of kilometres as some of the people I know.

My heart goes out to all these humans who went through unthinkable situations in the pursuit of happiness.

I know why you've spent money you didn't have to leave your country. You did it for your family. For your children's future. If you remained in your homeland, you wouldn't have spent that money, but your children would have starved. They wouldn't have the opportunity to a higher education.

***

Not every human is a bigot. I know many who would never dream to disconsider a person based on their nationality, the colour of the skin, sexual inclination, political views and so on.

I have many genuine friends whom I love very much. We resonate and cherish each other.

We cook and eat together. We talk and exchange untold stories of love or hate. I feel lucky to have Martine, for example, in my life.

She is an immigrant like me, born in France, a "superior" country. But she never ever made me feel inferior. Not one single humiliating word or condescending look.

I am grateful for people like her and many others. It is for them, the soulful, that I write.

I consider chauvinism lack of humanity. You can call it whatever you want. The truth is that we are losing our essence.

Racism and prejudice have been active since the beginning of time. So many lost their minds, their dignity, their faith and eventually their lives due to creatures without souls.

But after thousands of years, where are we going?

We are becoming more and more self-centred, superficial, and… empty.

We are not born blind. We chose not to see what's in front of us.

Nobody is racist from birth. We choose to discriminate.

I am not ashamed of being born in Romania. I am ashamed of being born in this era filled with so much racism but without any racists.

But I still love humans, and before judging and hanging, I give the benefit of the doubt.

Giving what I've been through, it's a conscious choice and I am proud of myself.

I owe Italy my future in England.

To Ceausescu, I owe my ability to survive and feel happy in a cage.

England is the country where the dream I never dared to dream came true.

Gene, saved my life when she helped me to move to the UK.

Martine, my dearest friend, is a human I resonate with on so many levels. Her constant support and understanding is priceless.

To you, my reader, I owe my status of a writer. I would be nothing without you.

Spread the love, amazing human being. Be generous and understanding. Make no mistake, either you believe or not, the universe will return the kindness.

**

If you liked this book, why not support the author by reviewing it on Amazon or Goodreads?

Also by Cristina G.

- Oranges at Christmas in a Communist Country
- Ten Years in Italy, Three Weeks a Human
- Humans Cursed by Geography in the Pursuit of Happiness
- Half My Age Plus Seven: **A Sinful Confession**
- Half My Age Plus Seven: **Too Good to be True?**
- It's Never Game Over
- iLive
- God is Weary
- Îmi Curg Mucii, Deci Exist
- Author for Life or for a Living? **Manifesto for Real Writers**
- **Childless: How to Cope with Endometriosis & Vulvodynia – Coming Soon**
- **Nobody Cries – Coming Soon**
- **Spinster or Scotch? – Coming Soon**
- Half my Age Plus Seven: **Book Trailer**

About the Author

Cristina G. was born in Romania during one of the harshest communist regimes that ever existed.

The tenth child of a farmer's family, she has six sisters and used to have four brothers, now only two.

Aged eight, she read *Les Misérables* by Victor Hugo and fell irremediably in love with books.

After living in Italy for ten years, in 2012, Cristina, encouraged by her brother, Sebastian, became a blogger.

In June of 2014, with the help of a British friend, Cristina moved to England. Here, although her expectations were not great, the dream she never dared to dream came true.

Cristina G. is now a registered author and dedicates her life to writing for soulful people.

Connect with the Author

If you'd like to know more about me and keep up-to-date with hot new releases, free promotions, giveaways, contests and much more, visit [AuthorCristinaG](#) & [While I Breathe I Hope](#).

For those who prefer the social platforms here are the [Google +](#) & [YouTube](#) and [Facebook](#) & [Twitter](#) accounts.

www.ingramcontent.com/pod-product-compliance
Lightning Source LLC
Chambersburg PA
CBHW020442220526
45464CB00002B/813